Contents

AF605118

A lot to offer

Never see a need without doing something about it.

Saint Mary MacKillop

Significant groups of people and individuals helped to shape the colonies in Australia during the 1800s. Of course, before European settlers started arriving, Aboriginal and Torres Strait Islander Peoples had been living on the land for almost 50 000 years.

The first European settlers were British, who arrived in 1788 to set up a **convict colony**. Some convicts did not want to work hard, and some tried to escape. Drought and **famine** marked these first years of European settlement. Hard years followed for the colony of New South Wales and the other colonies that were started. Individuals and different groups of people rose to the challenge of shaping the colonies. Their hard work and determination made the colonies better places to live and work for many people.

Did you know?
'Banjo' Paterson was a colonial poet. His poem 'The Man from Snowy River' was made into a successful film in 1982. It is still the tenth top earning Australian film of all time.

LET'S FIND OUT

- How did Aboriginal people contribute to the colonies?
- Which groups or individuals helped to shape the colonies?
- How did groups or individuals shape the colonies?
- Why would an individual or group decide to make a colony a better place to live?
- What hardships did people face in the 1800s?

---

convict a person who was transported to an Australian colony to serve out a prison sentence
colony a country or part of a country ruled by another country
famine a serious shortage of food

During the 1800s, life in the Australian colonies was hard, but individuals and groups worked hard to make life better. By the early 1900s, for example, Sydney was a thriving city.

Shaping the colonies

Australia would not be the nation it is today without the **contribution** of significant groups of people and individuals during the 1800s. These people were explorers, pastoralists or farmers, **entrepreneurs**, artists and writers, **humanitarians**, social, religious and political leaders, as well as Aboriginal people.

Some wanted a better life for a group or a community and fought for their rights. Others explored unknown areas of Australia, looking for new regions for settlement and farming. Edward Eyre and his Aboriginal guide, Wylie, for example, found a route between Adelaide in South Australia and Albany in Western Australia. Their journey covered more than 3200 kilometres. Today, the main highway linking the two routes is named the Eyre Highway.

Many of the people who shaped the colonies overcame challenges. Entrepreneur and social leader Mary Haydock, for example, was convicted of stealing a horse in England and transported to New South Wales in 1792.

Two years later, Mary married Thomas Reibey. He died in 1811, leaving her with seven children and many businesses. Mary ran all of the businesses, had fine buildings built in Sydney and made donations to schools. She appears on Australia's $20 banknote in memory of her contribution to New South Wales.

The country we live in today has been shaped by many groups of people and individuals. They had vision, energy, courage and concern for others. They saw something that needed to be done and did it.

Eyre and Wylie

contribution the role a person plays to bring about a result
entrepreneurs people who set up and run a new business
humanitarians people who help others and change society

Breakaway tasks

Remembering

1 List five roles played by the groups of people and individuals who contributed to a colony.

2 Discuss the four qualities of the groups of people and individuals who contributed to a colony.

Understanding

3 Explain how Edward Eyre and Mary Reibey helped to shape the colonies.

Applying

4 Based on the definition, discuss what sort of things a humanitarian might do.

5 Find out more about the explorer Edward Eyre. Make a time line of his life.

Analysing

6 Find out about the challenges Mary Reibey faced. Write a brief report on how she overcame them.

7 What might have been the consequences if the early Australian explorers had not found new land for people to live on and farm? Write a list.

Evaluating

8 Do you think Mary Reibey deserves to be on Australia's $20 banknote? Write a paragraph, giving reasons why or why not.

Creating

9 Find out more about another early Australian explorer. Write a song or poem about their life.

10 Create a slide show about the other people on Australia's banknotes. Include:

- who they are
- what they did
- why they deserve to be remembered in this way.

Stars of the past

Pemulwuy
Born about 1750 in Botany Bay, New South Wales
Died about June 1802 in Sydney

Contribution Pemulwuy was an Aboriginal leader. He belonged to the Bidjigal group who lived in the area now called Botany Bay. He was concerned about the Europeans taking his people's land. He united the Aboriginal groups living around Sydney to fight against the new arrivals. He showed the Europeans that his people would resist the new arrivals who were taking their land.

Remembered by the Sydney suburb, a book and a song.

Jane Franklin
Born 4 December 1791 in London, England
Died 18 July 1875 in England

Contribution Franklin was a social leader. While her husband was **lieutenant-governor** of Tasmania between 1836 and 1843, she worked to improve people's lives. She was particularly interested in the **welfare** of female convicts, and worked in Tasmania, Victoria and South Australia. She helped set up secondary schools and the scientific society that became the Royal Society of Tasmania. She was the first woman to climb Mount Wellington in Hobart.

Remembered by a college of the University of Tasmania.

---

lieutenant-governor the person in charge of a colony
welfare the health, happiness and fortunes of people

Henry Parkes
Born 27 May 1815 in England
Died 27 April 1896 in Sydney

Contribution Parkes was a political leader. He arrived in Sydney in 1839 and did various jobs. In 1894 he was elected to the New South Wales Parliament and his long career as a politician began. He was premier of New South Wales five times and did much to develop the colony. For example, he introduced nursing as a **profession**, and he made education free and **compulsory**. He also laid the groundwork for **Federation**, which occurred in 1901.

Remembered by the Canberra suburb of Parkes, the roads Parkes Way and Parkes Place in Canberra, and the town of Parkes, NSW.

Louis Ah Mouy
Born 1826 in China
Died 28 April 1918 in Victoria

Contribution Ah Mouy was an entrepreneur and a social leader. When he arrived in Melbourne in 1851, he heard about the discovery of gold and wrote a letter to his brother in China about it. It is believed that this letter caused many Chinese people to travel to the Victorian goldfields.

Ah Mouy was a very successful digger and used his fortune to open mines in Victoria and Malaya (now Malaysia). He was the leader of the Chinese community in Melbourne, and he was also an original director of the Commercial Bank of Australia in Melbourne. He contributed to the development of Victoria by providing people with employment and supporting his community.

Remembered as one of the first residents to trade in tea.

profession occupation or job requiring education or training
compulsory something you have to do
Federation the joining of the six colonies as the nation of Australia

Catherine Helen Spence
Born 31 October 1825 in Scotland
Died 3 April 1910 in South Australia

Contribution Catherine Helen Spence was a humanitarian. She arrived in South Australia with her family in 1839 and soon began writing to raise awareness of the needs of women and children. She published several books and started the first foster care program. She also supported the setting up of kindergartens, and was the first woman to stand for election to parliament in 1897. She fought for women's right to vote in South Australia, New South Wales and Victoria. Women in South Australia won the right to vote in 1894.

Remembered by a statue in Adelaide and a wing of the State Library of South Australia.

A.B. 'Banjo' Paterson
Born 17 February 1864 in New South Wales
Died 5 February 1941 in Sydney

Contribution Paterson first worked as a lawyer, but as a law student he wrote poetry, which was published in *The Bulletin* under the pseudonym 'The Banjo'. Banjo used his poetry to express his love for and pride in Australia. His ballads – including 'The Man From Snowy River' and 'Clancy of the Overflow' – were so popular with readers that they were published in 1895 in a collection of poems that is still in print today. He contributed to the development of New South Wales and an Australian identity by his celebration of Australian life.

Remembered on the Australian $10 banknote.

foster care placing children in need with families
pseudonym a made-up name, used to hide one's identity
ballads poems, often set to music, that tell a story

Breakaway tasks

Remembering

1 Write one contribution made by each of the individuals profiled.

2 Use the following words in sentences:
- humanitarian
- social leader
- entrepreneur.

Understanding

3 Make up a quiz for your classmates based on two profiles.

4 Compare the lives of Jane Franklin and Catherine Helen Spence. How were they similar? How were they different? Use a Venn diagram to present your findings.

Applying

5 Research Federation and Henry Parkes's role in bringing it about. Use your information to create a slide show.

6 Make up and play a game of Celebrity Heads about all of the people profiled.

Analysing

7 Imagine you are one of the six people profiled. Write a paragraph about how you would like to be remembered.

Evaluating

8 Debate the following statement: "Because Henry Parkes helped to bring about Federation, he deserves to be on an Australian banknote more than 'Banjo' Paterson."

9 Evaluate the contributions of the people profiled. Whose contribution do you think is the most significant and why? Write a response and compare your response with a partner's.

Creating

10 Research six other individuals who contributed to the colonies in the 1800s. Include at least one Aboriginal person, such as Simon Wonga or William Barak. Using the profile structure, make a poster of these six significant individuals.

An adventurer wanted

Many explorers risked their lives looking for farmland on the vast Australian continent. Without their contribution, the new colonies would not have survived. The future of the new colonies depended on feeding the hungry population. Farmers needed to grow crops and graze sheep and cattle to provide food.

The Blue Mountains around Sydney were the first major **obstacle** to finding farmland. In May 1813, Gregory Blaxland, William Lawson and William Wentworth cut their way through 80 kilometres of thick bush to arrive at the top of a mountain now called Mount Blaxland.

Below them was a valley, and beyond that was a grassy plain stretching to the horizon – land perfect for farming. Within 18 months, a road had been built over the mountains, and **free settlers** had started farming.

By the 1850s, explorers had travelled north and south of Sydney and around much of the coast, with free settlers following. But the middle of the continent was still a mystery, and no European had crossed it from south to north. A group called the Royal Society raised the money for a south–north crossing of the continent and advertised for applicants.

The journeys of the key explorers

obstacle something that stands in the way
free settlers people who chose to move to the colonies

WANTED: AN ADVENTURER

The Exploration Committee of the Royal Society seeks an adventurer to undertake and lead an expedition across the continent from the township of Melbourne in the south to the undiscovered north.

The successful applicant will be strong in body, able to withstand physical hardships and an excellent horseman. He must also be strong in mind, not afraid of danger.

He will inspire admiration and respect from those he commands, and trust and confidence from those to whom he reports. He will inspire others to do their best.

He must be able to observe his surrounding, the plants, animals, landscape and **inhabitants**, and report clearly and faithfully what he sees and hears. This expedition will be no **mean feat**.

He must lead other members of the expedition into the unknown and back again. Only serious applicants will be considered.

inhabitants people who live in an area
mean feat an expression that means 'a small task'

Breakaway tasks

Remembering

1 What were the explorers looking for?

2 List the tasks the Exploration Committee of the Royal Society sought an adventurer for.

Understanding

3 Summarise the information provided on page 10 about crossing the Blue Mountains.

4 Sort the qualities the adventurer needed to have under the following headings:
- Physical qualities
- Mental qualities

Applying

5 Do some research to find out who actually undertook and led the expedition, providing details, if possible, about:
- the man's name
- dates of birth and death
- what he did before the expedition
- why he got the position.

Analysing

6 Examine the map on page 10. While Aboriginal Peoples had trade routes that crossed the country, write why you think no Europeans had tried to cross the Australian continent from south to north before.

7 Discuss why the advertisement concludes with 'only serious applicants will be considered'?

8 Do you think a woman would have been able to undertake and lead this expedition as well as a man? Justify your answer.

Evaluating

9 Can you recommend some improvements to this advertisement? What other qualities would an adventurer need to have? Discuss your ideas.

Creating

10 Imagine you are planning an expedition into an unexplored part of the world. Decide where your expedition is heading and what you want it to achieve. Design an advertisement for the position.

Saint Mary

Before the 1860s, many children did not attend school, because their parents could not afford the fees.

Mary MacKillop knew what it was like to be poor. At 14, Mary started work to help support her family.

When she became a nun, she worked to provide free education to poor children in rural areas. By the end of 1869, more than 70 of Mary's nuns were educating children at 21 schools in South Australia.

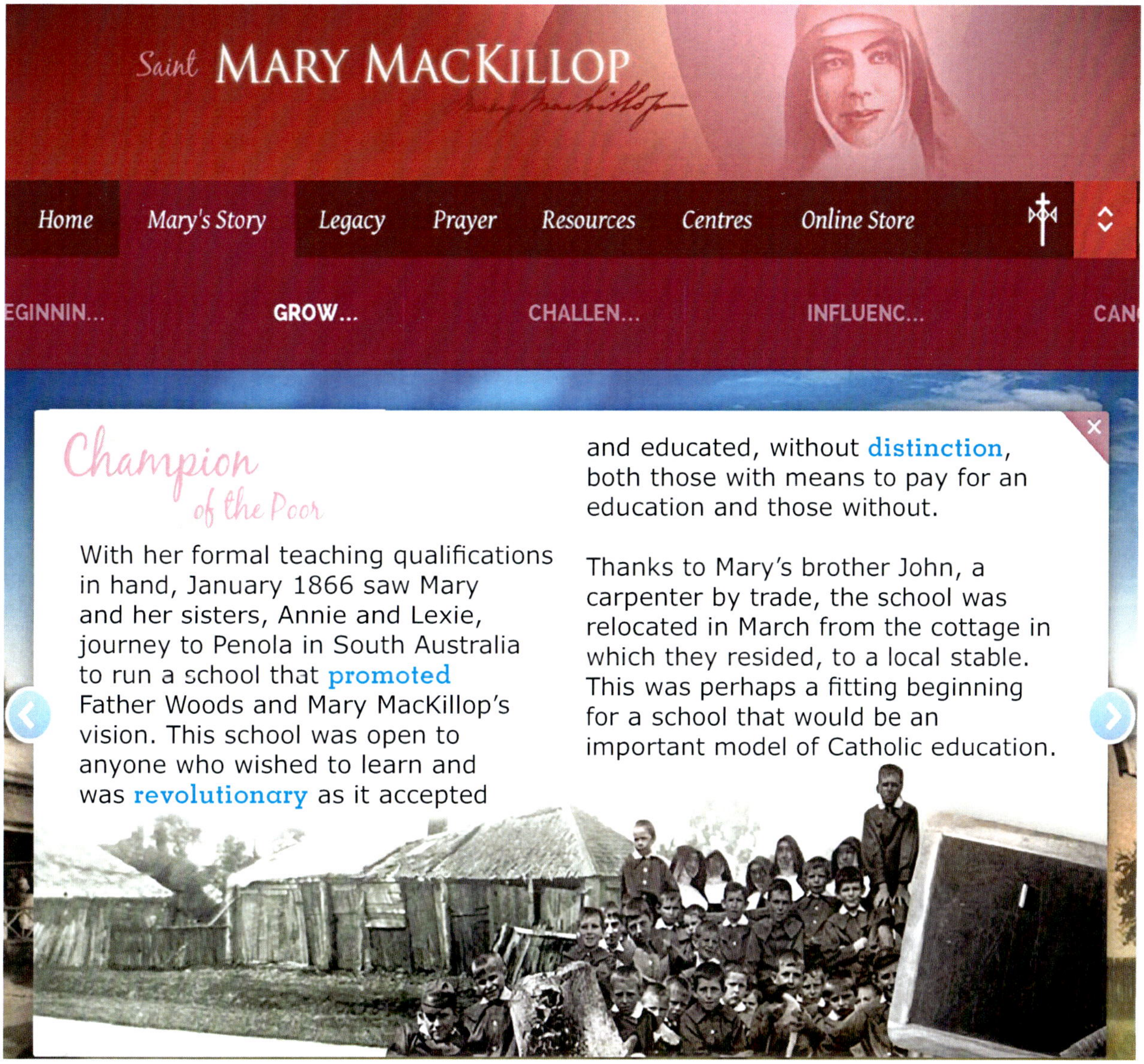

Saint MARY MACKILLOP

Home | Mary's Story | Legacy | Prayer | Resources | Centres | Online Store

EGINNIN... | GROW... | CHALLEN... | INFLUENC... | CAN

Champion of the Poor

With her formal teaching qualifications in hand, January 1866 saw Mary and her sisters, Annie and Lexie, journey to Penola in South Australia to run a school that **promoted** Father Woods and Mary MacKillop's vision. This school was open to anyone who wished to learn and was **revolutionary** as it accepted and educated, without **distinction**, both those with means to pay for an education and those without.

Thanks to Mary's brother John, a carpenter by trade, the school was relocated in March from the cottage in which they resided, to a local stable. This was perhaps a fitting beginning for a school that would be an important model of Catholic education.

promoted supported
revolutionary bringing about great change
distinction difference

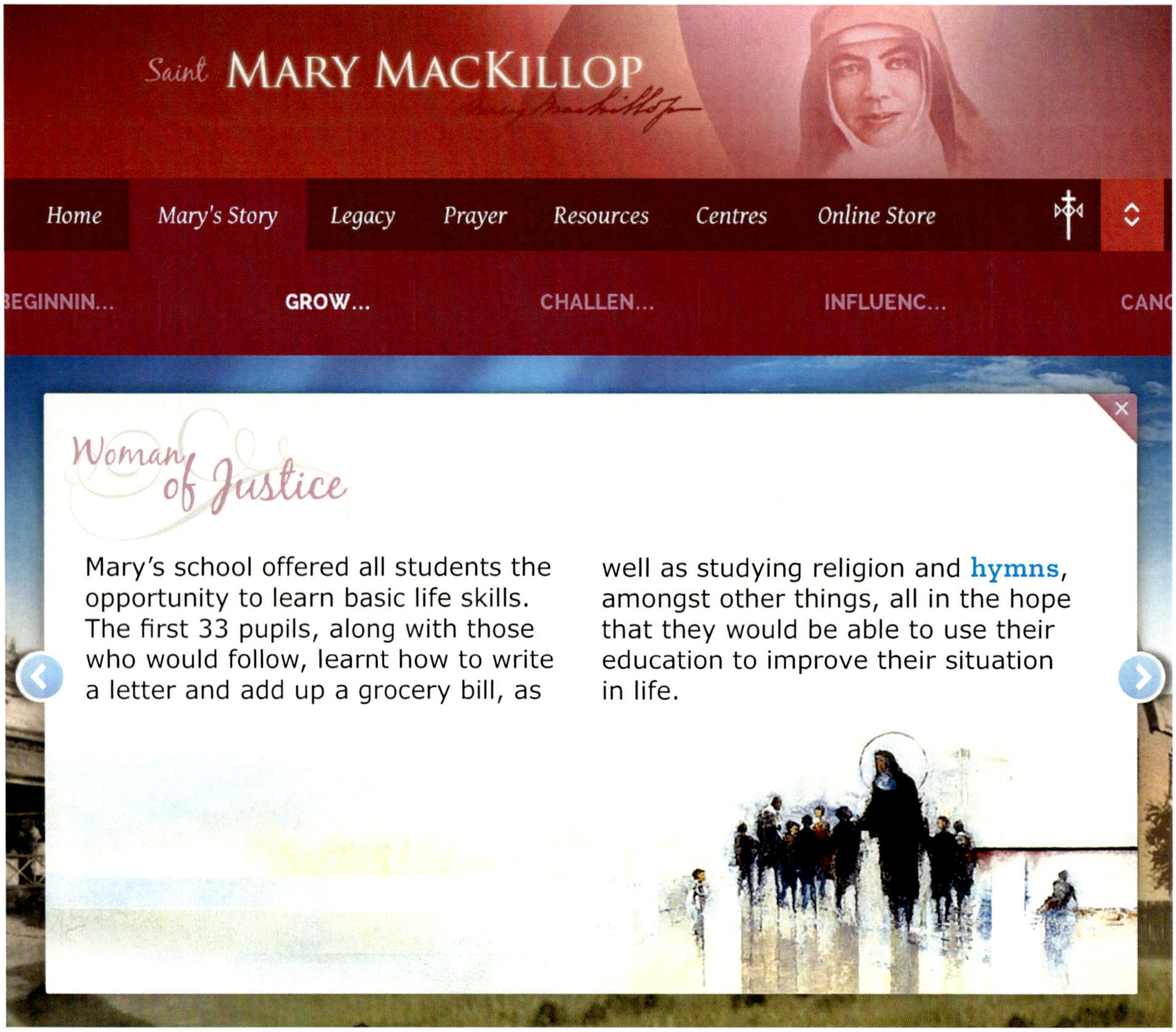

Saint MARY MACKILLOP

Home | Mary's Story | Legacy | Prayer | Resources | Centres | Online Store

BEGINNIN… | GROW… | CHALLEN… | INFLUENC… | CAN

Woman of Justice

Mary's school offered all students the opportunity to learn basic life skills. The first 33 pupils, along with those who would follow, learnt how to write a letter and add up a grocery bill, as well as studying religion and **hymns**, amongst other things, all in the hope that they would be able to use their education to improve their situation in life.

One way in which Mary MacKillop contributed to the shaping of the colony of South Australia was by providing education for all.

Mary MacKillop was declared a saint by Pope Benedict XVI on 17 October 2010. She is now known as Saint Mary of the Cross.

Statue of Mary MacKillop outside Adelaide Cathedral

hymns songs of praise for God

Breakaway tasks

Remembering

1 Who was accepted at Mary MacKillop's school?

2 List the subjects and tasks students were taught at Mary MacKillop's school.

Understanding

3 Identify the main point of both web pages. Rewrite each main point in your own words.

Applying

4 Use a Venn diagram to show the similarities and differences between what you learn today and what students learnt at Mary MacKillop's school.

5 Who was Father Woods? Find out more information about his life and how he knew Mary MacKillop. Write a short profile about him.

Analysing

6 Discuss what you think Mary MacKillop was hoping to achieve by opening schools.

7 Imagine you could meet Saint Mary. Write six questions and research possible answers. Conduct an interview with a partner.

Evaluating

8 Do you think what students learnt at Mary MacKillop's school would be useful to students today? Write a paragraph giving reasons why or why not.

9 What if Mary MacKillop and Father Woods had not opened this school? Consider the consequences for the students who attended the school, for their parents and for the colony of South Australia. Record your ideas.

Creating

10 Investigate Mary MacKillop's life. Do you think she deserved to be made a saint? Why or why not? Plan and create an oral presentation.

Strands in action

Core tasks

1 Research and present detailed profiles of two people from any of these significant groups during the 1800s: entrepreneurs, artists, religious or social leaders, Aboriginal and Torres Strait Islander Peoples, pastoralists, explorers and humanitarians. Include information about the colony or colonies they shaped, their contribution and how they are remembered today.

2 Research five new significant individuals who contributed to shaping the colonies during the 1800s. Write a short profile about each, including why you chose them. Choose one person and design the front and back of an Australian banknote that commemorates their contribution to a colony. Use significant elements from their life to decorate the banknote.

Extra tasks

1 Prepare a photo story with captions about one important person or one group from the 1800s.

2 Which person featured in this Student Magazine would you most like to meet and interview? Prepare 10 questions.

3 Choose one of the groups listed in Core task 1 and complete a KWL chart (what you know, what you want to know and what you have learnt). Consider as many different sources as possible.

4 Imagine you are writing a book about one of the significant groups listed above and how they shaped a colony. Write the table of contents, plan the content and give each chapter a title.

When you are preparing a **profile**, it is important to remember the difference between fact and opinion. The main purpose of a profile is to tell a person's life story by recounting the facts. When researching, you may find sources that comment on the person's life, instead of just recounting it. If you add a comment, make it clear that it is your opinion.